Thank you for studying

God's Word with us!

CONNECT WITH US
@thedailygraceco
@dailygracepodcast

CONTACT US
info@thedailygraceco.com

SHARE
#thedailygraceco

VISIT US ONLINE
www.thedailygraceco.com

MORE DAILY GRACE®
The Daily Grace® App
Daily Grace® Podcast

BIBLIOGRAPHY

Dennis, Lane T. and Wayne Grudem, ed. *The ESV Study Bible*. Wheaton, IL: Crossway, 2008.

Frame, John M. *Systematic Theology*. Phillipsburg, New Jersey: P&R Publishing, 2013.

Latreille, Christine. "How to make a DIY obstacle course outside." *Active For Life*. May 18, 2022. https://activeforlife.com/diy-obstacle-course/.

McLeod, Kimberly. "Sidewalk Chalk Paint." *The Best Ideas for Kids*. April 12, 2020. https://www.thebestideasforkids.com/sidewalk-chalk-paint/.

Merriam-Webster Online Dictionary. "Character." *Merriam-Webster*. Accessed September 1, 2022. https://www.merriam-webster.com/dictionary/character#dictionary-entry-1.

Merriam-Webster Online Dictionary. "Hope." *Merriam-Webster*. Accessed September 1, 2022. https://www.merriam-webster.com/dictionary/hope.

Perman, Matt. "What Is the Doctrine of the Trinity?" *Desiring God*. January 23, 2006. https://www.desiringgod.org/articles/what-is-the-doctrine-of-the-trinity.

Piper, John. "Regeneration, Faith, Love: In That Order." *Desiring God*. March 2, 2008. https://www.desiringgod.org/messages/regeneration-faith-love-in-that-order.

Super Teacher Worksheets. "Word Search Puzzle Generator." *Super Teacher Worksheets*. Accessed October 27, 2022. https://www.super-teacherworksheets.com/generator-word-search.html.

Ware, Bruce A. "'The Father, the Son, and the Holy Spirit: The Trinity as Theological Foundation for Family Ministry." *Southern Equip*. Southern Seminary, October 10, 2011. https://equip.sbts.edu/article/the-father-the-son-and-the-holy-spirit-the-trinity-as-theological-foundation-for-family-ministry/.

Theology For Me

BIG TRUTHS TO GROW YOUR FAITH

KATIE DAVIDSON

The study of God is fascinating and captivating, joyful and fun.

Table of Contents

Week 3

Week 4

Extras

How to Use This Resource

We are thrilled that you have decided to include *Theology for Me | Big Truths to Grow Your Faith* in your devotional library. This study was created to introduce young students of God's Word—specifically, those ages 10–14—to key fundamentals of systematic theology in a fun and accessible way.

Each day of this study includes:

- **SYSTEMATIC THEOLOGY TERM AND DEFINITION:** All terms and definitions can also be found in a glossary at the back of this resource.

- **KEY VERSE:** Key verses provide biblical context for each of the systematic theology terms.

- **EXPLANATION:** Each theological term is accompanied by daily content that explains the term with simple vocabulary and creative illustrations.

- **QUESTIONS:** Each entry includes three questions to foster understanding and application of the day's lesson.

At the end of each week of the study, you will also find:

- **ACTIVITY:** These fun activities are designed to help students better learn and apply gospel-centered truths to their daily lives.

○ MEMORY VERSE: Weekly memory verses help promote long-term Scripture memorization. See the extra on page 119 for practical tips to help students memorize Scripture.

While a 10–14-year-old could certainly go through this resource on their own, we recommend that this study be completed in the context of a discipleship relationship in which an older, more mature believer walks through the content alongside a younger believer to help them grow in their faith. With this in mind, throughout the study, we will refer to these two individuals as the DISCIPLESHIP LEADER and the STUDENT, though this discipleship relationship could take many different forms, such as:

○ DISCIPLESHIP LEADER: A parent, guardian, relative, pastor, youth group leader, teacher, or any trusted adult who leads a younger believer through this study.

○ STUDENT: A 10–14-year-old who commits to going through this study alongside a trusted adult.

However you choose to engage this resource, we encourage you to make the most of this discipleship relationship by sharing honest reflections and thoughts with one another. There is no right or wrong way to engage in *Theology for Me*, but here are a few tips to help along the way:

○ Begin each day's study with prayer, asking the Holy Spirit to guide you in truth and wisdom. You may also choose to pray at the end of each day's study, asking that the Spirit would help you apply the truth you have learned to your daily life.

○ Use any unknown words or concepts as an opportunity for students to learn how to look up and understand words that they do not know.

- o If a student is completing the resource on their own, it may be wise for a discipleship leader to check in on each day's lesson by discussing the day's questions with them.

- o It is okay for discipleship leaders to say "I don't know" to students' questions. Discussing and discovering these theological truths together can be a gift to both individuals.

Though the theological concepts in this booklet were written to be understood by students ages 10–14, some terms may not be immediately grasped. Do not become discouraged; this is okay! Discipleship leaders, it is great for us to teach our teens and pre-teens that sometimes we may have to rest in the tension between knowing and unknowing. Exposure to these biblical truths will plant seeds that God can water throughout the course of their lives.

To the students setting out on this study of systematic theology, we applaud your desire to know more about who God is and what He has done. And to the discipleship leaders walking with students through this resource, we are encouraged and delighted by your commitment to disciple younger believers in the truth of God's Word. Our prayer is that this resource will be one tool in your toolbox that helps you both love God. May your eyes and hearts be opened to the hope of the gospel, and may you come to saving faith in Jesus. The Daily Grace Co.® team is cheering you on!

May your eyes and hearts be opened to the hope of the gospel.

Introduction

CATEGORY: A group of people or things that share similar qualities.

READ ISAIAH 40:28

God is big. He is so big that He is beyond time and space. God is also all-powerful. He is so powerful that He created the world from His words. He crafted the birds of the sky, the fish of the sea, and the animals that roam the land. He knows how many grains of sand are on the seashore. He knows how many hairs are on your head. He is wise, patient, and beautiful. How will we ever understand all that God is to us?

The truth is, we will never fully understand God. And that is okay! However, as we study theology, which is the study of God, we will learn that He is much better than we could ever imagine. With every day and with every breath, we can spend our days getting to know all that we can about God through His Holy Word, the Bible.

Because God is so big, when we study Him, we do so in categories. Why categories? Categories help us see details and weave together themes that exist in God's Word and in the world. Categories also help us see similarities and differences, patterns and processes. For example, imagine you have a pile of Lego® bricks in front of you consisting of varying shapes and sizes. If you were to sort them by color, you might realize you have only a few yellow pieces and many more blue and green pieces. If you were to sort by shape, you might see that you

Who God is changes everything.

have many more long pieces and fewer shorter pieces. Studying Lego® pieces in categories can help you understand the entire makeup of your Lego® set. Likewise, as we study who God is by considering different categories, one at a time, we begin to better understand His character and how He works. This system of studying God in categories is called systematic theology.

Studying who God is in categories also helps us better understand God's plan for our world. As we look around at our everyday lives, it is not hard to see that the world is broken. We scrape our knees, endure hurtful words, and sometimes feel sad and confused. Waffles burn, and pets pass away. But as we study God in categories, we learn more about His character, His works, and all that He has made. Doesn't this sound amazing?

This study will teach you about the foundations of the Christian faith. But don't be fooled. The study of God is not boring. The study of God is fascinating and captivating, joyful and fun. As you continue, some words may feel big and intimidating at first. But don't worry! If you are a Christian, you have a Helper, the Holy Spirit, working within you to help you understand who God is. And even if you are not yet a Christian, the Holy Spirit is working to help people like you see how much you need God (John 16:7–11). By the end of this study, you will know God better than you did before. And who God is changes everything.

Memory Verse

In the beginning was
the Word, and the Word
was with God, and
the Word was God.

JOHN 1:1

What is Theology?

THEOLOGY: The study of God, His Word, and His works.

READ JOHN 17:3

Do you know your best friend's favorite color? What about his favorite flavor of ice cream? Or her favorite YouTube channel? Likely, you know facts about your best friend because you've spent so much time with him or her. Because you care for her, you know her likes and dislikes, what she loves and doesn't love. In the same way, we get to know God through studying about Him and spending time with Him.

This is theology. Theology is studying God, His Word, and His works. In this way, everyone is a theologian because everyone has thoughts and beliefs about God. Therefore, our job is to make sure our personal theology comes from God's Word, which is what we call the Bible. Why? God gives us His Word so that we may learn about Him. We get to discern theology straight from the source—the very Word of God. You may have many questions about God: *Why does He do what He does? Is God ever joyful? Does God truly love us? Did God create penguins and seahorses?* All of these questions are answered through the study of theology. As we study the Bible, we get to know God and discover answers to some of our biggest questions. We find the truth and encouragement we need to give us peace in our everyday lives.

The ability to know God is our joy and privilege! Not only is it a joy for us to get to know God, but God also enjoys being in a close relationship with His people — that is why He sent Jesus! You will learn more about this soon. But for now, as we begin to learn about theology for ourselves, we can remember that our study of theology deepens our worship and awe of the God we love. As we study Him, we gain His good wisdom about the world. God gives us the humility to say "sorry." God gives us the strength to make it through hard days. God gives us the wisdom to say "yes" to what is good and "no" to what is bad. There are endless benefits to studying theology! But most of all, by studying theology, we learn who God is — a good Father, whose love will never fail us.

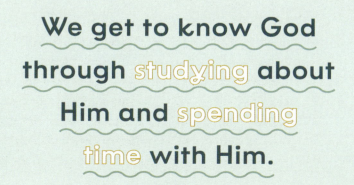

We get to know God through studying about Him and spending time with Him.

By studying **theology,** we learn who God is.

DISCUSS TOGETHER

1. In your own words, how would you describe God?

2. Theologians are men and women who study the Bible. Would you consider yourself a theologian?

   a. *Hey, discipleship leaders! Remind your students that anyone who studies God is a theologian!*

3. If you could ask God one question today, what would that be?

The Trinity

THE TRINITY: The Trinity is the one true God in three persons—God the Father, the Son, and the Holy Spirit. All three persons of the Trinity are equal and eternal but have unique roles.

READ JOHN 14:9–10

There is one true God. God exists in three persons: the Father, the Son, and the Holy Spirit. The Father, Son, and Spirit are called the Trinity, and the word "Trinity" means "three in one." The Trinity is perfectly united, which means that the persons of the Trinity do not work against each other or apart from one another. The Father, the Son, and the Holy Spirit all have the same goals and plans. They never argue. They are in agreement on every decision. The Father, the Son, and the Holy Spirit always work together.

The three persons of the Trinity exist equally. This means that the Father, Son, and Spirit share the same nature. They are all fully God. There will never be a time that the persons of the Trinity will stop being God. Because the persons of the Trinity are God, they are all eternal. They have always existed, and they will always exist (Genesis 1:2, Psalm 90:2, Hebrews 13:8).

Yet the three persons of the Trinity also exist uniquely. God is the Father (Philippians 1:2), Jesus is the Son (Matthew 16:16), and the Holy Spirit is the Spirit (John 14:26). God will always be the Father, Jesus will always be the Son, and the Holy Spirit will always be the Holy Spirit. And the three persons of the Trinity also have unique roles. They all have done, are doing, and will do different things. For example, God the Father is the One who sent Jesus to us (John 3:16). Jesus the Son is the One who died on the cross for us (Luke 23:33–49). And the Holy Spirit is the One who opens our eyes to our need for Jesus (John 14:16–17).

But even though the persons of the Trinity exist uniquely, they all make up one God. They are not separate Gods. Each person of the Trinity is God. As Deuteronomy 6:4 tells us, "The Lord our God, the Lord is one." And God Himself declares, "See now that I alone am he; there is no God but me" (Deuteronomy 32:39).

If you're a little confused, you are not alone. The Trinity is a difficult concept to understand! But the mysteries of the Trinity show us just how amazing God is. Even though we can't wrap our minds around the Trinity, we can allow the truths of the Trinity to encourage our worship of God. God is the one true God! There is no one like Him! The ways He works are incredible! Praise the Father, the Son, and the Holy Spirit for being more than we could ever imagine.

Even though the persons of the Trinity exist uniquely, they all make up one God.

The mysteries of the Trinity show us just how amazing God is.

DISCUSS TOGETHER

1. Who are the three persons of the Trinity?

2. What did you learn by studying the Trinity?

3. Name the role of each member of the Trinity.

The Father

THE FATHER: The first member of the Trinity. God is a Spirit who is infinite, eternal, and unchangeable. He is the One who initiates salvation. Salvation was His plan from eternity past.

THE FALL: Refers to Adam and Eve's disobedience in the garden of Eden through which sin entered the world.

READ MICAH 7:18

What are some characteristics of a good dad? You may say loving, supportive, funny, or hard-working. Fathers here on earth can be great, but they are also flawed. No father on earth is perfect. Sometimes, they mess up and fail their families. However, God the Father never fails. Nothing can hinder His plans, and He always brings His plans to completion.

Furthermore, like a good dad plans for the well-being of his family, the Father set forth a plan for the redemption of the world. In simple words, redemption means to restore what is broken—and because of sin, our world is certainly broken. But thankfully, the Father had a plan to fix all that sin broke from the very beginning.

See, in the beginning, the Father spoke the creative words that brought the universe into existence. By the Father's creative hand, and through the Son and the Spirit (Genesis 1:2, Psalm 104:30, Colossians 1:15–16), the stars were hung in the sky, the oceans roared with their first waves, and the birds sang their first song. He made mountains and trees, lions, squirrels, and even mankind. His creation was perfect, just as He was.

Unfortunately, mankind chose to disobey God, and sin entered the human race. This is called the Fall. And it affects us even today as we experience a world that is far from perfect. We get sick, lose our favorite things, and sometimes get angry at our parents. Like a horrible disease, sin has infected every corner of the world. But there is great news. The Father will not allow sin to remain forever. The Father's plan of redemption has a good ending. Tears will be no more. Instead, the Father's love and splendor will fill the earth. All things will be made new.

Until the Father restores the world, He offers us glimpses of heaven through His Son, Jesus. The Father is responsible for beginning the process of our rescue from sin. He draws normal, sinful humans to Himself and introduces them to Jesus. And when sinful humans trust in Jesus, their sins are forgiven, and their sinful nature is washed away. No one can come to Jesus without being called by the Father (John 6:44). This truth prompts us to live in thankfulness! If you place your trust in Jesus, that means that the Father sought you to join His family. He chose to give you the greatest gift of all—Himself! In the Father's care, we find the greatest joy and the most delightful rest.

Even when situations do not make sense or we can't see the end of a rainy day, we can trust that the Father's plans are always for our ultimate good (Romans 8:28). God's plan will bring Him glory and allow us to experience His presence in a way that gives us peace no matter the troubles we may face. We can also rest in the fact that nothing we do—none of our mistakes—can stop our heavenly Father's plan. We can let go of the pressure to be the best or the smartest or the most athletic as we rest in the Father's love. We can take a deep breath, relax our minds, and trust that the Father is in control.

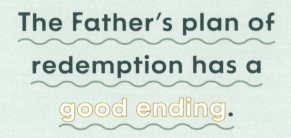

The Father's plan of redemption has a good ending.

DISCUSS TOGETHER

1. How would you describe God the Father in your own words?

2. Today we learned about the Father and His good plan for the world. Why can you look forward to the future God has prepared?

3. Open your Bible and find Psalm 146:6. What do you worry about? Why can you trust that the Father is in control?

The Bible

BIBLE: The holy, true, and authoritative Word of God.

AUTHORITY: The right to give orders and require obedience.

HOLY: Moral wholeness and perfection; the absence of evil.

READ 2 TIMOTHY 3:16–17

Ever since the very beginning of our world, God has used His words to create and care for life on earth. Scripture tells us that "God said, 'Let there be light,' and there was light" (Genesis 1:3). God spoke and created giraffes, sharks, and parrots—every animal you can think of! He created the flowers and the mountains, the stars and the sea.

God's words carry the power to accomplish anything He wants. Why? Because God is all-powerful and has the authority to carry out anything He desires. Authority means that God has the right to give orders and require the obedience of His creation. Because God made the world, He determines how it operates. God uses His words and authority for good, not evil. God uses His words to share His love.

Did you know that we have access to God's powerful words every day? Over the course of hundreds of years, God used ordinary humans to record messages to His people. God gave these people His words and instructed them to write them down. Those words, put together and bound in a book, make up the Bible. Scripture tells us that the Bible is breathed out by God—a story told by God Himself. The Bible is one big story, made up of hundreds of smaller stories that all tell of God's plan to rid the world of sin through His Son, Jesus, and one day make His creation perfect again.

By the Bible's instruction, Christians learn about God and how to please Him with our words, actions, and hearts. The words found in Scripture are not like those in your favorite book. God's Word is holy, true, and authoritative. The Bible is holy because God is holy—He is perfect. God's Word is true because God cannot tell lies. His Word is authoritative because He is the Lord of all.

Truly, we cannot have a personal relationship with God without knowing His Word. As we read the Bible, we read words with the same power and authority that were used to create the universe. And these words help us know God and love Him more. The Bible is a gift from God—better than any birthday gift or Christmas present—that teaches us God's love, trains us for good works, and gives us hope for our future.

God uses His words to share His love.

God's Word is holy, true, and authoritative.

DISCUSS TOGETHER

1. What is the Bible?

2. How do we know we can trust what the Bible says?

3. Why is it important for followers of Jesus to read the Bible?

Man

MAN: Mankind was created in the image of God, but that image is stained by sin and can only be restored by Jesus's sacrifice on the cross.

CHARACTER: Traits or features that set a person apart.

READ GENESIS 2:7

In the beginning, God created the birds of the sky, the creatures of the ground, and all the fish in the sea. But then, God created His most favorite creation of all—mankind. God called all of His other creations "good," but He called mankind "very good." Why were humans God's favorite?

Scripture tells us that God made man in His own image. Even some of the best Bible teachers are unsure what exactly this means, but we do know that God made man different from any of the animals. God formed man out of the dust of the ground and breathed life into him. Isn't that cool? God's own breath gave us life! God also gave man qualities that reflect His character. And most importantly, God gave man the ability to relate to and get to know Him.

God provided the garden of Eden to be home for the first man, who was named Adam. But this home was not yet complete. God said, "It is not good for the man to be alone" (Genesis 2:18), so God put Adam to sleep and took a rib from his side. Out of this rib, God created a woman named Eve. Like Adam, Eve was also created in God's image. God loved her, just as He loved Adam. He instructed the pair to work as a team and invited them to help care for His creation. God gave them authority over all the other animals. He instructed them to farm the land and fill the earth with more and more people. Adam and Eve lacked nothing and lived every moment in God's love. For a while, man and woman lived in the garden of Eden in peace.

Unfortunately, the peace between man and God did not last very long. The devil, in the form of a sneaky snake, slithered into the garden to separate man from God. And unfortunately, His plan worked. We will read more about this soon! Long story short, Adam and Eve disobeyed God and sparked the flame of sin, which spread like wildfire through generations and generations of humans and continues still today. The relationship between God and mankind became broken. However, as we continue learning about theology, we will learn all about God's great plan to create something beautiful from what was broken. God loves us too much to leave us in sin. Though mankind separated themselves from God, God planned to go to great measures to bring them back home.

God loves us too much to leave us in sin.

God gave
man the ability
to relate to
and get to
know Him.

DISCUSS TOGETHER

1. How does God describe mankind? How would you say that God describes you?

2. Read Genesis 2:18. What did God mean when He said, "It is not good for the man to be alone"? Why do you think we need one another?

3. What do you think the garden of Eden would have been like? How is it different from the world today?

God Created Everything

Have you ever thought about how amazing it is that God created everything? The birds, the fish, the sky, the grass—everything in the world was created by Him and for Him! For this activity, we will try to create like God creates!

Below, you will find a list of exotic creatures of God's creation. Some swim in the sea, some roam the earth, and others fly in the sky. Each one of them is especially unique and crafted intentionally by God. Let's explore some of His creations!

Animals

1. Narwhal
2. Platypus
3. Markhor
4. Peacock
5. Komodo Dragon
6. Snowy Owl
7. Axolotl
8. Blue Parrotfish
9. Red Panda
10. Cheetah

Activity:

Pick an animal (or several) from the list on page 34 and research it by visiting your local library or going online. As you're researching, consider the following questions:

1. Where does your animal live?

2. What do they eat?

3. What does their skin look like? Do they have scales, feathers, fur, or something else?

4. What is the size of your animal?

5. What makes this animal unique?

Now that you've researched your animal, it is time to start creating! Draw or create this animal using items around your house (e.g., construction paper, cardboard, markers, glue, pom poms, wrapping paper, etc.). Try to make them as close as possible to the photos you found as you researched your animal.

Once you have created your animal, answer the questions below.

1. What does the uniqueness of your animal teach you about God?

2. Was it difficult or easy to create your animal? How does this make you appreciate God's ability to speak creation into existence?

HEY, DISCIPLESHIP LEADERS!

Consider reading Psalm 148 together after you finish creating.

Memory Verse

If you confess with your mouth, "Jesus is Lord," and believe in your heart that God raised him from the dead, you will be saved.

ROMANS 10:9

Sin

READ ROMANS 6:23

Have you ever been sick? When you're sick, unwelcome germs come into your body and cause you to cough or sneeze. We can think of sin as a sickness that has invaded the world. Sin is not just evil thoughts or actions; it is unbelief in God. It is not doing what God asks of us, either actively or passively, in thought, action, or attitude.

You may be wondering, *How did sin enter our world?* That's a great question. When God breathed life into the world, He said it was "good" (Genesis 1). God's creation had no flaw. He created mankind to be in a perfect relationship with Him. God loved Adam and Eve, cared for them, and even allowed them to share responsibility in His creation. But unfortunately, the devil, in the form of a sneaky snake, desired to destroy God's creation. So, the devil tricked Adam and Eve into eating fruit from the only tree God instructed them not to eat from — the Tree of the Knowledge of Good and Evil. Adam and Eve wanted the knowledge and power that was only meant for God to have. And so they disobeyed God and ate from this tree, and their disobedience caused sin to enter the world. Today, we often call this event the Fall.

How did God feel about sin entering His perfect creation? God hates sin, and sin cannot be found in His presence since He is holy and perfect. Because of this, God gave Adam and Eve specific consequences for their actions: They would lose their home in the garden of Eden, farming would be tiresome and difficult for the man, and childbirth would be painful for the woman. Relationships would be strained with arguments and frustrations. And worst of all, sin separated Adam and Eve from the God they loved. Through Adam and Eve's disobedience, sin and brokenness flooded the world and infected every corner and crevice.

Every single person in history is a slave to sin. Being a slave to sin means that we cannot do anything that pleases God. Since sin is our natural state as humans, this means that your grandparents, your parents, your neighbors, and your friends all have this dreadful disease called sin. And even young children struggle with sin. From a young age, we are rude to our parents. We take what is not ours. We use our words to hurt others. Because of the Fall, things like death, disease, lies, and bullying slithered into the human experience. Sin is the reason that countries war against one another. Sin is the reason families argue. Sin is the reason for selfishness. But the worst part about sin is that sin affects our relationship with God (Isaiah 59:2).

Sin separates us from God. Though God despises sin, He loves us too much to distance Himself forever. The story of the Bible is about God rescuing His people from sin. In the next few weeks, we will learn all about His great rescue mission. This is a mission with one hero—a hero named Jesus.

The story of the Bible is about God rescuing His people from sin.

DISCUSS TOGETHER

1. Describe sin in your own words.

2. Where do you see sin in the world?
   Where do you see sin in your own life?

3. Sometimes, sin may feel right or good.
   For example, you may feel like someone
   deserves to hear unkind words. How can you
   know when something is wrong or a sin?

The Son

THE SON: The second person of the Trinity who accomplished salvation for sinners through His life and death.

READ PHILIPPIANS 2:8–9

If you have ever used a smartphone or tablet, you have likely used an app. An app is the name for the software that runs games, movies, and music on a smart device. With so many apps on one device, software engineers had to come up with a simple way to show the user where each app was located on the home screen. So, they did this by coming up with something called icons. Icons are the little pictures you see on a device's screen. These icons represent the various apps on a device. This is a very simple analogy to help explain how the Son represents the Father. Like an icon represents an app, so the Son, Jesus, represents the Father to the world.

Jesus was always the central focus of the Father's plan to give peace to the world. It was by the Son that the heavens and the earth were created (Colossians 1:15–16). Then, as sin began to take over God's good creation, Jesus was the exciting future promised to God's people. The problem was always sin, and Jesus was always the solution. How did He solve the problem of sin? Great question!

Jesus's home is in heaven in the presence of His Father. But He left that home to come to earth as a little baby. This little baby was just like babies today—a little boy in need of His mother. He cried and cooed and needed diaper changes. But Jesus was different in two important ways. The first is that this baby was the Son of God. His mother was a woman named Mary, but He had no biological father. The Holy Spirit created Jesus inside Mary's belly. The second way that Jesus is unique is that He never sinned. He never stole from His friends or yelled at His parents. He was always respectful and always kind. Jesus was fully human and fully God. He likely felt sunburn and bee stings. Jesus was betrayed by His friends and was misunderstood. But even in all of these temptations, He remained sinless.

Throughout Jesus's time on earth, He healed diseases, brought the dead back to life, and preached fascinating messages about the kingdom of God. The Son was not selfish like we are but sought only to make His Father known. Unfortunately, many people did not recognize Him as their Savior. Though completely innocent, Jesus willingly died a brutal death on the cross. On that tragic day, He experienced death—the punishment of sin—so that we could come near to the Father in relationship with Him.

Three days after Jesus's death, He rose from the dead. After spending forty days with His disciples, He ascended into heaven, proving His identity as the Son of God. Jesus's death and resurrection make it possible for us to have a relationship with the Father. Jesus now reigns as King in heaven, but one day, He will return to establish His kingdom. He will obliterate all evil and tenderly wipe away the tears of the hurting. If we confess that Jesus is Lord and believe in Him as our Savior, we are not only free from sin; we have a hope-filled future to look forward to in heaven with Him.

The problem was always sin, and Jesus was always the solution.

DISCUSS TOGETHER

1. What is the Son's role in the Father's plan for redemption?

2. Describe the Son's time on earth. What did He do? What did He experience? How can Jesus relate to you?

3. Jesus shed His own blood so that you can be free from sin and called a son or daughter of God! You are fully known and loved by Him. Consider whether you have confessed that "Jesus is Lord" and believed in your heart that "God raised him from the dead" (Romans 10:9). If you have, write a prayer thanking Jesus for His sacrifice. If you haven't, consider whether that is something you would like to do now.

Redemption

READ JOHN 3:16

REDEMPTION: Redemption is the sinner being freed from sin.

What are the qualities of a good king? You may think of qualities like kindness, patience, courage, or even being someone who is adventurous and fun! The Bible calls Jesus the King of kings. He is the best King who perfectly cares for His kingdom. Since Jesus is a good King who cares for His people, He embarked on a rescue mission to save His people from slavery to sin.

You may be wondering what the term "slavery" means here. It means that sin is like a chain on our hearts that pulls us in the opposite direction of God. As hard as we try, we cannot loosen the chains by ourselves. That's why we need Jesus! Jesus, the best King, came to break these chains and bring us to freedom. Redemption is the sinner being freed from sin.

To better understand redemption, let's take a look at a story in the Old Testament. Have you ever heard of the book of Exodus? Exodus tells the story of when God's people were in slavery in Egypt. The Egyptians mistreated them and forced them to do brutal, awful, and tiring work. God's people cried out to Him, and God listened. To prove His love for His people, God did miraculous things for the Israelites. He sent plagues upon the Egyptians—filling their land with frogs and booming thunderstorms. The water even turned to blood! Finally, Egypt's king, the Pharaoh, released God's people from slavery. In this story, God set His people free—He redeemed them from their bondage!

However, though God's people were saved from slavery in Egypt, God's people were still slaves to sin. Because of their sin, the Israelites wandered in the wilderness for forty years, waiting and waiting and waiting for a place to call home. Unfortunately, God's people wanted more than just a relationship with Him. Though God was their King, they wanted their own country and a human leader to call king. Even so, God provided for them each day. God rained bread from heaven and gave them water from a rock. But they were still unsatisfied.

Throughout the Old Testament, God's people continued to face challenges because of their disobedience. They had terrible kings and troublesome priests. Sometimes they were even conquered by neighboring countries. God promised them a better King would come. One day, their troubles and tears would disappear in the peace of the coming King. All of their sins would be forgiven. They would finally be able to rest their heads at night with no fear.

This promised King is Jesus, who ultimately sets all God's people free from slavery. However, Jesus's work to redeem us does more than release us from our slavery to sin; it also frees us to enjoy spiritual blessings that can only come from a relationship with Him. This includes eternal life, righteousness, adoption into God's family, and peace with God, to name a few. For those of us who follow Jesus, we are rescued and safe in the kingdom of the greatest King—King Jesus.

This promised King is Jesus, who ultimately sets all God's people free from slavery.

DISCUSS TOGETHER

1. Why does God want to free us from sin?

2. How does understanding the story of the Israelites finding freedom from Egypt help you understand how Jesus frees us from sin?

3. How is Jesus the best King?

Atonement

ATONEMENT: Christ accomplished salvation for God's people through His sinless life and obedient death on the cross.

READ 1 PETER 3:18

What happens when winter changes into spring? All of a sudden, the grass becomes green, flowers begin to bloom, trees bud with bright new leaves, and animals come out of their hiding. What was once a dreary winter is now a vibrant spring. In a similar way, when Jesus Christ, the Son of God, was born as a baby in a manger, mankind's hope began to bloom. The Savior had finally burst forth to take away humanity's sin and bring us back into a relationship with God.

But why did Jesus come to earth as a baby? He was born to make atonement for us. This big word—"atonement"—means that Jesus came to accomplish salvation for God's people. And He did this through His sinless life and obedient death on the cross.

As we learned a few days ago, Jesus lived a sinless life. This means that as Jesus walked on earth, He was completely obedient to God with every step He took and every word He spoke. Jesus was so obedient and so selfless that He took it upon Himself to solve mankind's biggest problem: sin. God is good and perfect, and therefore, He despises sin. Sin pulls God's people away from Him. Therefore, God desired to make a way for humans to be forgiven of sin so that they could come close to Him again. But sinful humans could not solve the problem of sin. Jesus, being perfect, was the only One able to rescue God's people from the darkness of sin and bring them into the light of God.

And so, on a gloomy Friday, Christ surrendered His life and died on the cross. His death was not accidental but was a part of God's good and perfect plan. As Jesus hung on the cross, He carried the sins of all mankind. Instead of allowing God's people to die for their sins, Jesus experienced the pain and punishment that we deserve. Through Jesus's sacrifice, those who trust in Him as Lord and Savior have their sins forgiven and removed from them completely. God does not view us as enemies, covered in sin, but as sons and daughters, washed clean in Christ.

Although our hope blossomed through Jesus's life, Jesus's victory over death is not like a season. Seasons change. They come and go. But the atonement that covers our sin and brings us into a right relationship with God will never fade away. If we trust Christ as our Savior, we can rest knowing that the peace Jesus provides lasts forever. With these truths in mind, let our praises grow! God has done great things for us. Atonement reminds us that in Christ, we are dearly loved and fully forgiven by God.

The atonement that covers our sin and brings us into a right relationship with God will never fade away.

Atonement reminds us that in Christ, we are dearly loved and fully forgiven by God.

DISCUSS TOGETHER

1. What is the cost of sin? (*Hint: Read Romans 6:23.*) Why do you think God feels so strongly about sin?

2. What does Jesus accomplish for us through atonement?

3. Because Jesus forgives our sins, does that mean we can keep sinning? Why or why not?

   a. *Hey, discipleship leaders! This is a big question. Here's a sample of how you may answer this question!*

   "If we sin because we know that Jesus has forgiven us, we are taking advantage of God's kindness. A person who trusts in Jesus receives a new heart. We no longer desire to sin, but instead, we want to please Jesus with our every word and every action. Sometimes, we will mess up along the way! That is okay, but in our mess-ups, we must bring ourselves back to Jesus. He is sure to help us learn from our mistakes and forgive us."

Gospel

HOPE: To trust with confident expectation of good.

GOSPEL: The good news that salvation comes by grace alone through faith in Jesus Christ alone.

READ EPHESIANS 2:8–9

Did you have a favorite bedtime story as a little kid? There is something about a good story that pulls us in and fills us with wonder. The gospel is the best story of all. Unlike a good bedtime story, the gospel does not only fill our heads with characters and action-packed details—the gospel is a story that changes our lives. The gospel is the good news that salvation comes by grace alone through faith in Jesus Christ alone. It is the story of lost people finding hope and an eternal home.

So far this week, we have learned individual pieces of the gospel. We have learned that man was born in the perfect image of God. Unfortunately, Adam and Eve disobeyed God, and through their disobedience, sin entered the world. Sin destroyed God's perfect creation. Suddenly the effects of sin could be seen everywhere—in broken relationships, in disobedience to God, in evil kings, and in harsh words. But God loved us way too much to leave us in brokenness.

God sent His only Son to live among humans—to teach and to love them. God's Son, Jesus, was fully God and fully man. He was perfect and never sinned against God. Yet this perfect man died a painful death on the cross to save us from sin. And three days later, He rose again from the grave and defeated sin! Through Jesus, God showed His great love for us, deeper than any ocean and higher than the highest mountain peak. God's love for us cannot be measured. And in this, we place our faith. (We will learn more about faith soon!)

The gospel reminds us that sinners are saved by grace through faith. Grace is the undeserved favor of God toward a sinner. And faith is believing in what you cannot see. More specifically, as followers of Christ, faith is trusting in Jesus Christ for the forgiveness of sin and the promise of eternal life with God. We exercise faith when we make a personal decision to trust Jesus for salvation based on what we know about Him from the Bible.

If these definitions seem confusing, don't worry! We will dive more into these topics later. For now, however, we can recognize that everyone on earth has a choice—we can either believe that Jesus died on the cross to pay for our sins, or we can choose to pay for our own sins by suffering God's just punishment.

If you accept the truth that Jesus died for you, this means that you make Jesus the King of your life. It means you accept that He is smarter than you, that He cares better for you than you care for yourself, and that He has control over the world. Trusting in Jesus means you believe that Jesus is the main character in your story, not yourself. This can be hard and difficult to do, but it is the best choice you will ever make. Jesus promises that if we trust in Him, the ending of our story will be good. Why? Because our story will be filled with Him.

The gospel reminds us that sinners are saved by grace through faith.

DISCUSS TOGETHER

1. How is the gospel the greatest story ever told?

2. If you had to describe God's love for you to a friend, how would you describe it?

3. Do you believe the gospel is a truth or a lie? Why do you say that?

Learning Redemption Through Chalk Paint

Hey, discipleship leaders! This activity will help teach students what it means that Jesus has washed our hearts clean of sin. In this activity, you will create chalk paint with your students and then use this paint to splatter on a section of sidewalk. The splatters will represent sin, and at the end of the activity, you will wash these splatters away, just as Jesus washes our sins away.

First, let's make some chalk paint!

Supplies Needed

1. Plastic or paper cups or a muffin tin
2. Thick paint brushes
3. 4 Tablespoons of cornstarch (per color)
4. 4 Tablespoons of water (per color)
5. 1 Piece of sidewalk chalk (per color)
6. A grater or plastic bag and a rolling pin
7. A hose or some pitchers of water

Instructions:

1. Pick a color of sidewalk chalk you'd like to use, and then grate that piece of sidewalk chalk into a bowl. If you do not want to use a grater, don't worry! You can put your piece of chalk into a plastic bag and roll it with a rolling pin until you get one tablespoon of chalk dust. Do this with each color you plan to use.

2. Mix together the cornstarch and water. Then add in the chalk dust. Mix until well-blended. If your chalk does not seem thin enough to splatter, feel free to add a few more drops of water!

3. Pour the mixture into cups or a muffin tin for easy transportation outside.

4. Read the following prompts, and instruct your students to make a splatter on the sidewalk if they have ever been guilty of any of these common sins. This splatter can be singular, or they can splatter as much as they want each time. You can get creative with this! Try making each sin a different color of paint or switch up colors throughout the activity!

Prompts to Read

- Make a splatter if you've ever taken what isn't yours.
- Make a splatter if you've ever disobeyed your parents.
- Make a splatter if you've ever wanted something that a friend has had.

○ Make a splatter if you've ever cheated on a game or a test in school.

○ Make a splatter if you've ever called someone a mean name.

○ Make a splatter if you've ever loved something more than you love God.

○ Make a splatter if you've ever complained about something.

○ Make a splatter if you've ever refused to share.

○ Make a splatter if you've ever told a lie.

○ Make a splatter if you've ever made a selfish decision.

○ Make a splatter if you've ever failed to be thankful.

○ Make a splatter if you've ever been jealous of someone else.

5. After they are done with their splatters, say this:

"Wow, that's a lot of splatters! This sidewalk used to be clean, but now it's messy. This is what sin does to our hearts. As we go throughout our lives, sins continue to make our hearts messier and messier. But if we trust in Jesus, He cleans our hearts of sin and gives us a fresh start."

6. Use a hose or pitchers of water to wash away the chalk paint from the sidewalk. After the sidewalk is clean, say this:

"Now our sidewalk is clean! Jesus's forgiveness cleans our hearts. Throughout our lives, sin will continue to make life messy. That is why we must continue to ask Jesus for forgiveness. As we grow in our faith, we will learn to better turn from our sin and rest in Jesus's grace."

Memory Verse

But God, who is rich in mercy, because of his great love that he had for us, made us alive with Christ even though we were dead in trespasses. You are saved by grace!

EPHESIANS 2:4–5

Grace

GRACE: The undeserved kindness of God toward the sinner.

READ EPHESIANS 2:4–5

What is the best gift you have ever received? Maybe it was a toy at Christmas or a birthday present or maybe even a vacation! Whatever the gift was, you probably did little to deserve it, right? It was given from the kindness of those who love you. In the same way, grace is the undeserved kindness of God toward the sinner. God gave us this gift of grace when we were the messiest, most disrespectful versions of ourselves. This means that God forgave our sins even though we did not deserve that forgiveness, and He continues to give us undeserved kindness throughout our lives on earth. This does not mean that everything will always go our way or that we will never experience pain, but it does mean that God will be with us every step of the way.

In order to extend His grace to us, God sent His Son, Jesus. Jesus is God's grace in the form of a man. He walked alongside people just like you and me. He healed their sicknesses, drew near to the broken-hearted, and taught them about the coming kingdom of God. These people were not special. They did not earn this attention from Jesus. Instead, Jesus, the King of kings, was delighted to spend time with sinners and the outcast. Jesus gifted His presence freely out of His love. And then, Jesus extended even more grace to the people of Israel and to Christians throughout all time. Jesus Christ died on the cross to forgive the sins of anyone who believes in Him. While we deserve death, Christ gives us life. Though we deserve punishment, we gain a reward in Christ.

Grace is a gift that is given to us over and over again, every single day. For those who trust in Jesus as their Savior, the mistakes of yesterday, today, and tomorrow are washed away. We do not have to be embarrassed about our mess-ups. We do not have to hide in shame. Instead, we can admit our mistakes to God in confidence that He will forgive us and help us become more like Christ tomorrow than we are today. God's grace is a gift that never runs out. It is the best gift we will ever receive — better than any Christmas toy or birthday present or fun vacation. Through Jesus, we have experienced the kindness of God.

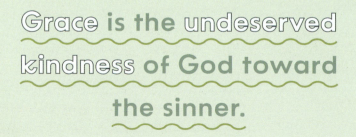

Grace is the undeserved kindness of God toward the sinner.

Grace is a gift that is given to us over and over again, every single day.

DISCUSS TOGETHER

1. Why does God give grace to sinful humans?

2. Is grace given to us once, or is it given to us over and over again throughout our lives?

   a. *Hey, discipleship leaders! This may be a confusing question for students at first! But it is a great chance to encourage your students that God's grace is not a one-and-done situation. As God's children, we receive His kindness (grace) in every moment of our lives. As we mess up throughout our lives, He is quick to forgive those who come to Him in humility and honesty. Try reading James 4:6–8 as you discuss!*

3. Think about a time when you did not want to forgive someone else. How does God's grace to you encourage you to give grace to others?

Regeneration

READ EZEKIEL 36:26

What would happen if you suddenly became a superhero? What would your powers be? How would your life be different? Your old self would be a thing of the past, and your new way of life would be filled with excitement. In a similar way, if someone is in Christ, they are a new creation (2 Corinthians 5:17). How does this happen? That's a great question!

When you accept Christ into your heart, it is because He has already begun to work in you. This is the work of regeneration. Regeneration is God's work in a believer's life to give them new spiritual life. We can think of this as a "new birth." This means that when regeneration takes place, your spiritual life begins! Like a baby learns to crawl and eat and walk, you learn to see the world with new eyes—eyes that see as Jesus sees. You may see someone in need and desire to help them. You may see someone lonely and remind them of God's love. You may see someone who does not know Jesus and desire to introduce them to Him.

The Bible tells us that before we come to know Christ, our hearts are like a stone—hard, stubborn, and unable to understand or respond to God's love. But through the Holy Spirit's work of regeneration, our hearts become flesh—soft and compassionate (Ezekiel 36:26). As we read God's Word and begin to know Him better, our words, our actions, and our thoughts begin to change. We receive a new life that is marked by faith, love, and obedience (1 John 5:1–4).

Faith is the first sign that we are followers of Christ. As we discussed at the end of last week, a life of faith is marked by trust in Jesus Christ for the forgiveness of sin and the promise of eternal life with God. It involves knowing who Christ is and what He has done. This is done through knowing Scripture and agreeing with what it has to say about Christ.

Love is the second sign that we are followers of Christ. The love that marks our new life in Christ comes from God. As followers of Christ, God calls us to love Him and others (John 13:34, 1 John 4:20). We love God and others out of God's love for us and through the power of the Holy Spirit (Galatians 5:22–23).

Obedience is the third sign of a transformed heart. Obedience is choosing God's way over the ways of the world. In order to obey God, we must know what He says! This is why reading the Bible is so important. The Holy Spirit works inside our hearts to teach us God's Word and put what it says into action.

The great thing about regeneration is that once you are made new, you can never be your old self again! You may have moments of doubt or of disobedience, but the Holy Spirit will always remind you of your new life in Christ. This is because the work of regeneration is not accomplished by us but by our good God in heaven, who never fails.

When you accept Christ into your heart, it is because He has already begun to work in you.

DISCUSS TOGETHER

1. Think about the ways that you have grown throughout your life. For example, as a baby, you could not move on your own, then you began to crawl, and then eventually, you walked! In what ways might you "grow up" as a Christian throughout your life?

2. How might God's Word and the Holy Spirit change your words, your actions, and your thoughts to honor Jesus?

3. Find a Christian adult who you know and ask them this question: How is your life different now that you follow Jesus?

   a. *Hey, discipleship leaders! This might be a perfect time to share a little bit of your personal story of faith with your students. You might consider sharing how you came to saving faith and how your life is different now than it was before you became a believer.*

Faith

FAITH: Trusting in Jesus and believing in His promises today.

READ HEBREWS 11:1

Imagine that you are blindfolded in the middle of an obstacle course. The person you trust most is giving you directions for when to move forward and when to turn. Because you trust them, you have faith that they will help you get through the obstacles, right? Though you can't see them or what's around you, you trust in their character to carry you through. This example helps us understand our faith! Faith is trusting in Jesus and believing in His promises.

Though today we cannot see Jesus with our eyes, the Bible tells many stories of when Jesus walked beside people just like you and me. He was born as a little baby, fully man and fully God. He grew up, just like you grow up. Yet Jesus never sinned. Because Jesus was fully God while He was a human, He had all the wisdom, all the knowledge, and all the power of God. With His power, He healed and forgave sins. But sadly, many did not have faith in Jesus. These people arrested Jesus and sentenced Him to a brutal death on the cross. But don't worry. Though Jesus's death was unbearably sad, His death on the cross forgave you of your sins. And then, three days after Jesus died, something miraculous happened! He rose from the dead, gained victory over sin, and eventually returned home to heaven.

Faith is deciding that we believe Jesus really is the Son of God, who died for our sins and promises eternal life with God, exactly like the Bible tells us. Just as we imagined at the beginning, sometimes life is like an obstacle course. You may be afraid. You may feel lost. But if you decide to put your faith in Jesus, He is your trusted friend who is always by your side. And one day, Jesus will finish what He started. He will rid the world of all obstacles and all evil. Finally, the earth will be at peace. Those who have faith in Him will live in endless joy! That means that our faith brings us hope. Faith in Jesus means we trust that He is with us today and that He has a good future prepared for us in heaven.

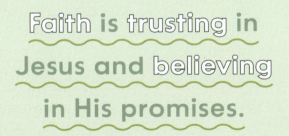

Faith is trusting in Jesus and believing in His promises.

Faith is deciding that we believe Jesus really is the Son of God.

DISCUSS TOGETHER

1. Everyone has faith in something. For example, you may have faith that your parents will pick you up from school or that the cookie you eat will taste just as delicious as you remember. What are other things you have faith in? How does this help you understand faith in God?

2. Why can you trust that Jesus is real, even though you cannot see Him?

3. How does faith in Jesus give you hope for a good future with Christ?

Repentance

REPENTANCE: Intentionally turning away from sin and turning toward God in obedience to His Word.

READ LUKE 5:32

Sometimes in life, we get lost, right? Maybe you lose sight of your parents in a store. Maybe you can't find your way around school. No matter the situation, when we are lost, we turn around and find the right direction! This is the same with our relationship with God. Following Jesus requires us to realize that we are lost in sin. Because of the Fall, we were born this way—as people lost in our sin. And to find our way, we must head in God's direction. As we learned earlier, repentance is intentionally turning away from sin and turning toward God in obedience to His Word.

In order to repent, we must know what sin is! How do we know what sin is? The Bible and the Holy Spirit tell us! Earlier in this study, we learned that sin is "not doing what God asks of us, either actively or passively, in thought, action, or attitude." As we continue to read the Bible, grow in our understanding of God, and be convicted by the Holy Spirit, we begin to understand just how sinful we really are. We may be tempted to hide our sin or feel ashamed, but recognizing our sin is the beginning of repentance!

After we recognize our sin, the next step in repentance is to admit that God's way is much better than our own way. This requires humility. Humility is recognizing that we need God's help. In fact, God tells His people that He will listen and provide for them if they will "seek His face" (2 Chronicles 7:14). What does this mean? It means that repentance involves prayer. Prayer is talking to God. God loves to listen to His children and is quick to forgive when we come to Him with humility.

Finally, the last step of repentance is to turn away from sin and walk in the Spirit, relying on Him for strength. Because God is good, we can trust that His way is better than our own way. If we are ever confused about what God's way is, we can find the answers we are looking for in the Bible. Remember, we can always ask God to show us the right direction. We are not alone! Because the Holy Spirit guides and directs us, we do not need to fear!

We can think of God as our home—the place where we belong. Through repentance, God is inviting us to come back home to Him, to return to the place where we are loved and safe.

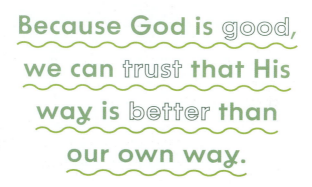

Because God is good, we can trust that His way is better than our own way.

Through repentance, God is inviting us to come back home to Him.

DISCUSS TOGETHER

1. Have you ever been lost? How did it feel? How might it feel to be lost from God?

2. When we repent, we recognize that God's way is much better than our own way. Why might it be hard to follow God's way over our own way?

3. What is something that you need to repent from? Follow these steps of repentance to ask God to forgive you.

   a. *Recognize your sin: What sin have you committed against God that you need to ask forgiveness for?*

   b. *Admit that God's way is better: How is God's way better than your own way? How can God help you overcome your mistake?*

   c. *Turn away from sin: Take a moment to read 1 Corinthians 10:13. Based on this verse, how are you able to turn away from sin?*

Justification

JUSTIFICATION: God declaring sinners not guilty.

READ ROMANS 8:1

Have you ever been inside a courtroom? A courtroom is a big, fancy room where adults make important decisions. This is where citizens are declared "guilty" or "innocent" of their crimes. If a person is found guilty, they may have to pay money or go to jail. Either way, there is always a consequence for crimes.

When it comes to sin, the Bible says we are all guilty. Therefore, we all deserve to be punished for our crimes, and Scripture tells us that the punishment of sin is death (Romans 6:23). But when Jesus died on the cross, He took our punishment so that we could be declared innocent. This is justification!

Let us slow down to first understand why we are guilty. We are guilty because when sin entered the world through Adam and Eve, it infected every human being. Now, sometimes we lie, we act selfishly, we steal, or we call others mean names. The list goes on and on! It doesn't take long to see just how guilty we are.

Jesus, on the other hand, is completely innocent. He never once sinned before God. He obeyed God perfectly. He was always generous, always patient, and always kind. Jesus deserved a reward, not a punishment. But God chose to give Jesus the punishment we deserve. Though we deserve to die for our sins, Jesus died in our place. Jesus took on our guilt so that we could be seen as innocent in God's eyes.

Because of Jesus's sacrifice, followers of Christ can come close to God. Now when God looks at followers of Christ, He does not see the sin of their past, but instead, He remembers the innocence of Jesus. Isn't that good news? That is why the story of Jesus is called the gospel. The word "gospel" means "good news."

How should we live in light of this good news? We should be thankful! With every breath we take and with every song we sing, we can give thanks to God for setting us free from sin. As we worship, we can bring others into this freedom, too, because everyone has sinned and is guilty, in need of God's grace.

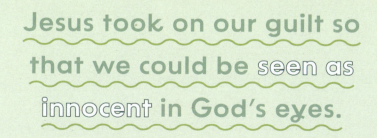

Jesus took on our guilt so that we could be seen as innocent in God's eyes.

Because of
Jesus's sacrifice,
followers of
Christ can come
close to God.

DISCUSS TOGETHER

1. If you had to describe justification to a friend, how would you describe it?

2. List out all the sins you've committed in the past day, week, or month. If you follow Jesus, you can rest assured knowing that He has removed every one of these sins. To represent how He has done this for you, take a marker or crayon and scribble through each of the sins listed.

3. Take a moment to consider whether you have ever confessed that "Jesus is Lord" and believed in Christ for your salvation (Romans 10:9). If so, praise Him for all He has done for you. If not, consider whether this is something you would like to do and discuss it with a trusted Christian adult, such as your discipleship leader.

Obstacle Course

On Week 3, Day 4, we discussed faith using an illustration of an obstacle course. Now, you have the opportunity to put faith into action by building an obstacle course of your very own! To illustrate what faith is like, students will be blindfolded and led through the course by following the instructions of their discipleship leaders.

Can you make it through the obstacle course?

STEP ONE: Build the Obstacle Course

The most fun part of completing an obstacle course is building it! This obstacle course can be created inside or outside. It can be as complicated or as simple as you would like it to be. Please remove any items that would be a tripping hazard from the area you choose. And, of course, be safe!

A few things for discipleship leaders to keep in mind:

1. Determine the beginning and end of your obstacle course.

2. While you are building, remember that students will be blindfolded while navigating the obstacle course, so keep this in mind while creating obstacles!

3. This is a great opportunity to let students be creative and build their own obstacles. However, you may

have to guide their creativity, as some obstacles may be too difficult to complete blindfolded.

Here are a few ideas of household items that would be great to use when creating your own obstacle course. However, these are only suggestions. Feel free to get creative!

- **Pool noodles:** Pool noodles can be used to mark off an area to jump or to create a walkway, or they could be stood up vertically and anchored to the ground to weave in and out of.

- **Extra pieces of wood:** Lay a scrap piece of lumber on the ground to create a balance beam to walk across.

- **Cardboard boxes:** Use cardboard boxes to create a tunnel or cut them into stepping stones to walk across.

- **Hula hoops:** Hula hoops are great to step through or crawl through!

- **Bats and balls:** Use bats and balls to add some extra fun to your obstacle course. Maybe you have to hit the ball off a tee or shoot a soccer ball into a goal.

Remember: If you do not have these items above lying around, don't worry. An obstacle course can be simply having your student navigate your house while blindfolded, trusting in your directions.

STEP TWO: Find a Blindfold

Use a handkerchief or another cloth to create a blindfold for your student. They will be unable to see while you are giving directions to navigate them through the obstacle course. Make sure they cannot see.

STEP THREE: Complete the Obstacle Course

Instructions for discipleship leaders:

1. Secure the blindfold on your students and set them at the starting point.

2. Use simple directive instructions to help students navigate the course. For example, you might say, "Take two steps to the right. There will be a tunnel straight ahead. Get down on your knees, feel for the tunnel, and crawl through it."

3. Encourage students along the way, especially as they get closer to the end!

4. For extra fun and competition, set a timer and see how fast students can complete the course!

Instructions for students:

1. Your discipleship leader will blindfold you. The point of this obstacle course is to navigate the obstacles without seeing them. So fight the urge to peek beneath the blindfold!

2. As you navigate the obstacles, listen carefully to your discipleship leader's instructions and follow their guidance exactly. Don't be afraid to ask questions. They can answer them.

REFLECTION QUESTIONS

Discipleship leaders, after you and your students have had your fill of the obstacle course, ask them these questions.

1. Why did you listen to what your discipleship leader said as you navigated through the obstacle course? Why did you trust their directions?

2. How can God see life better than you can see? Why can you trust what He says?

3. How does God give you instructions to navigate life?

Memory Verse

I have been crucified with Christ, and I no longer live, but Christ lives in me. The life I now live in the body, I live by faith in the Son of God, who loved me and gave himself for me.

GALATIANS 2:20

The Holy Spirit

THE HOLY SPIRIT: The third person of the Trinity who applies the work of salvation to the hearts of believers.

READ JOHN 14:26

Consider the wind. Can you grab onto the wind? Can you trap the wind in a box? No, the wind cannot be seen. Yet, after a windstorm has passed, you may find broken branches lying on the street or toys tossed around the backyard. Though you cannot see the wind, you can certainly find its effects. We can think of the Holy Spirit in the same way. Unlike Jesus, the Holy Spirit does not have a physical body, but He does have a home. The Holy Spirit lives inside the hearts of every believer — teaching, guiding, and transforming them into the image of Christ.

As we discussed in the first week of this study, the Holy Spirit is a member of the Trinity. Therefore, He has existed from the very beginning of time (Genesis 1:2). In the Old Testament, God used the Holy Spirit to demonstrate His faithfulness to His people. Even though sin caused God's people to rebel, God's love never left them. In the Old Testament, God's Spirit worked differently than it does today. The Holy Spirit would only come upon a person to do specific works that continued the Father's good plans and purposes. For example, the Holy Spirit worked in the hearts of kings and prophets to lead God's people in wisdom.

What does the Holy Spirit do now? Great question! When Jesus conquered death and rose from the grave, He returned to His home in heaven. But before Jesus left, He encouraged His disciples that they would not be alone. He said, "I am with you always, to the end of the age" (Matthew 28:20). Jesus is with us through the Holy Spirit. Everyone who trusts in Christ as their Savior receives the Holy Spirit. He comes to live in your heart to guide you and lead you to be reflections of Jesus in a broken world.

Throughout our lives, the Holy Spirit will give us the wisdom to determine right and wrong. The Holy Spirit even helps us pray when we don't know what to say. When we are afraid, scared, or confused about what to do next, we can remember that we are not alone. If you have trusted Jesus as your Savior, the Holy Spirit lives within you.

The Holy Spirit lives inside the hearts of every believer.

If you have trusted Jesus as your Savior, the Holy Spirit lives within you.

DISCUSS TOGETHER

1. How would you describe the Holy Spirit in your own words?

2. How does someone receive the Holy Spirit?

3. What is something that the Holy Spirit has taught you?

   a. *Hey, discipleship leaders! This could be a great time to share how the Holy Spirit has impacted your life—helped you turn from sin, taught you something in God's Word, or guided you in decision-making.*

Adoption

ADOPTION: Bringing the sinner into the family of God so that now God is his or her heavenly Father.

READ ROMANS 8:16–17

The word "family" sparks different feelings in everyone. Some people get excited to talk about their families, while other people's families cause them sadness and even anger. The truth is, no family on earth is perfect. No matter where you fall in these categories, there is good news for anyone who trusts in Jesus. Once we are saved by Jesus, we gain a brand-new family. Though we still belong to our earthly moms and dads and brothers and sisters, we are also welcomed into the heavenly family of God through adoption! This means we also become sons and daughters of God, and He becomes our Father.

Because we are adopted by God, this means that we are chosen by Him. We are not chosen because we are the best or most athletic or smartest; we are chosen simply because God loves us. Like a good dad delights in his kids, God loves to spend time with His children. He is never annoyed by our prayers or frustrated by our questions; instead, God wants us to bring every feeling and desire to Him. We can come to Him when we feel sad, happy, frustrated, or excited. No prayer is too big, and no request is too small to bring to our Father in heaven.

Adoption gets even better! Not only do we gain a new family, but we also gain a new home. Our true place of belonging becomes Christ's kingdom in heaven. It is no secret that the world we live in today is not perfect. Friendships disappoint us, things break, and storms make us shudder in fear. But for those who trust in Christ, we have a better future ahead. Our life on earth is temporary, but the joy we will experience in our true home—Christ's kingdom—will be never-ending. In Christ's kingdom, we will never feel sad or lonely or angry. Instead, we will feel constant love and constant peace in the presence of our Savior, Jesus.

When we are tempted to lose hope today, we can remember that we are adopted sons and daughters of God, chosen by Him so that we may live for Him.

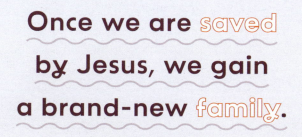

Once we are saved **by Jesus, we gain a brand-new** family.

For those who trust in Christ, we have a better future ahead.

DISCUSS TOGETHER

1. What does being a "child of God" mean? With this in mind, how do you think God feels about you?

2. Do you deserve to be in God's family? Why or why not? What did God do to ensure that you are called His son or daughter?

3. Now that we know we can bring any prayer to our Father in heaven, what prayer would you like to bring to Him today? Do you have any feelings you need to tell Him about? Do you have any sins you need to own up to? Take a moment to come to God as a child would come to a father.

Sanctification

READ GALATIANS 2:20

Have you ever planted a seed? After a few weeks of watering it daily and giving the soil plenty of sunshine, you will start to see leaves begin to grow out of the once-barren soil. With care and dedication, through weeks and months, that plant will continue to grow and grow. It may sprout flowers or even fruit! Our faith is much the same. When we decide Jesus is the Lord of our life, our faith begins small. But as we read the Bible and are taught by God's Holy Spirit, our faith begins to grow. And it continues to grow throughout our lives so that one day, our faith that started out just like a small seed will grow into a mighty tree of faith. Sanctification is growing more and more like Jesus through the power of the Holy Spirit.

What is so cool about sanctification is that the Holy Spirit helps us look like Jesus. We will not physically become like Jesus, but our hearts will be transformed to look more like His heart. Because Jesus is God, without the presence of sin, Jesus lived in perfect love, joy, peace, patience, kindness, goodness, faithfulness, gentleness, and self-control. These characteristics are called "the fruit of the Spirit" (Galatians 5:22–23).

Can you imagine what life would be like if everyone around you was perfectly kind, perfectly gentle, perfectly joyful, and perfectly at peace? The good news for Christians is that the Holy Spirit works in our hearts to bring about the good fruit of the Spirit in our lives. With the Holy Spirit, we will better love our parents and our friends. We can be patient when it is hard. We can be faithful when we want to give up. This is not because we are good but because God's Holy Spirit makes us good.

As we grow in our knowledge of God and His Son, Jesus, we become like fruit-filled trees in the middle of a desert. We will grow to be able to share God's peace, His kindness, and His love with our friends and our families. But one of the best things about sanctification is that God does not wait until we are fully mature Christians to use us for His good purposes. In fact, the Bible is filled with story after story of God using young Christians or even kids to share His love and faithfulness with the world. Scripture tells us that "he who started a good work in [us] will carry it on to completion until the day of Christ Jesus" (Philippians 1:6). This means that God never gives up on those in His family. He will continue to grow and teach and transform us until we finally meet Jesus in heaven.

God never gives up on those in His family.

Sanctification is growing more and more like Jesus through the power of the Holy Spirit.

DISCUSS TOGETHER

1. How does God transform Christians into the image of Christ?

2. What is the fruit of the Spirit? Who makes it possible for this fruit to grow in our lives?

3. Read about a few Bible characters who were young but were also used by God to do big things. To start, you can read about King David in 1 Samuel 16:1–12. Even though David was young, he was still chosen by God to be king. Though you are young, how might God use you in your home or at your school?

Perseverance

PERSEVERANCE: Once someone begins to follow Christ, they will never stop believing in Him; their new life in Christ will continue into eternity.

READ ROMANS 8:38–39

Did you know that some people run twenty-six miles at once? This is called a marathon. To celebrate finishing such a long race, runners typically receive a medal! The fastest marathon time in history is about two hours. Can you imagine running for two hours straight? Often, in the middle of running long distances, it can be hard to continue. Your legs may begin to hurt, or you might feel tired. But when marathon runners are tempted to quit, they remember the medal at the end of their race and find the strength to keep going.

In the same way, Christians will face trials and temptations throughout life, but we endure by remembering the prize at the end of the race—spending forever with our Savior, Jesus Christ. Perseverance means that once someone begins to follow Christ, they will never stop believing in Him; their new life in Christ will continue into eternity.

To understand perseverance, we must first understand the meaning of eternity. Eternity is the end goal of a believer — it is our medal at the end of the race. The Bible says that one day, Jesus will return and make the earth brand new. There will be no more evil, no more sadness, and no more fear. Instead, we will live in the peaceful presence of Jesus for all our days. When we are tempted to give up, we can remember the joy that awaits us in heaven. Because there is a good end to our story, we can press on.

Just like runners receive a medal at the end of a race, Christians are rewarded with eternity in heaven. But thankfully, we do not have to persevere through this life on our own. When Jesus died on the cross and forgave our sins, He gave us God's Holy Spirit. With the Holy Spirit in our hearts, God is always near. Together, the Holy Spirit and God's Word teach and guide us to live in a way that honors Him.

God gives us strength when we feel like giving up. When we stumble into sin, He picks us up with grace and forgiveness. In fact, the Bible tells us that nothing in the entire world is able to separate us from the love of God that is in Jesus (Romans 8:39). No matter the circumstance, we can remember that we have everything we need to run our race well, for the prize at the end of the race is a treasure worth more than gold. Our prize is Jesus.

Eternity is the end goal of a believer — it is our medal at the end of the race.

The prize at the end of the race is a treasure worth more than gold. Our prize is Jesus.

DISCUSS TOGETHER

1. What do you think eternity with Jesus will be like?

2. How does the Holy Spirit help us persevere?

3. When you have a hard day and feel like giving up, what truths from God's Word can help you persevere?

   a. *Hey, discipleship leaders! You can help your students brainstorm truths from God's Word by sharing some of your favorite Scriptures, discussing encouraging Bible stories, or looking up some of these suggested verses together: Deuteronomy 31:8, Joshua 1:9, John 16:33, and Romans 5:3–5.*

Glorification

GLORIFICATION: The end goal of every believer. Believers will be free from sin and will be transformed to have glorious bodies like Christ.

READ 2 CORINTHIANS 3:18

When you look in the mirror, what do you see? You see yourself as others see you. You can tell your eye color, the curve of your nose, and the details of your haircut. A mirror reflects whatever is in front of it. In the same way, when we experience glorification, we will perfectly reflect Jesus. When others see us, they will see the light of Jesus. We will be holy like He is holy. We will be at peace like He is at peace. We will be good like He is good. We can think of glorification as the end goal of a believer. One day, believers will be free from sin and will be transformed to have glorious bodies like Christ.

Earlier in this study, we learned that humans are made in the image of God. Yet sin caused that image to be dirtied and disfigured. Now, we are imperfect representations of God. Yet we have the opportunity to chase after holiness now, even though we are still surrounded by sin. As Christians, we will face many difficulties throughout our lives, but we can face them with hope, knowing our future reward is better than we can even imagine. When glorification happens, God will return the world to how it was originally intended to be. Our bodies will be made new—free from sin, free from disease, and free from pain. Our hearts will be joyful and at rest.

But the best gift of glorification won't be having a new body or being sinless (though these will be great!)—it will be what our new bodies and sinlessness will allow. Because we will be completely washed of evil and given the perfection of Christ, we will spend eternity with God and His Son, Jesus. This means that even on our worst days, we have hope. When our bodies fail us or our hearts stray from God, we know that our bodies and our circumstances are only temporary. One day, we will be made new. One day, we will be free from sadness and anger and anxious feelings. One day, we will be at peace with the Savior we love, Jesus.

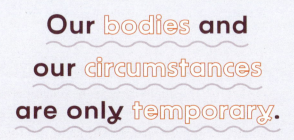

Our bodies and our circumstances are only temporary.

One day, we will be at peace with the Savior we love, Jesus.

DISCUSS TOGETHER

~~~~~~~~

1. Read Revelation 21:3–7. What do these verses say will one day happen to the world? Where will God dwell? Why is this good news?

2. How does the promise of glorification give you hope on your worst days?

3. Our minds cannot begin to imagine how it will feel to be free from sin and live forever in the presence of Jesus, but we can try! What do you think it will be like to live with Jesus in a perfect world?

The Great Commission

The theology terms we have learned about in this study are like the puzzle pieces of our faith. They come together to teach us all about who God is and what He has done for us! If we had to make a list of everything He gives us, that list would be never-ending. But God's greatest gift to us, by far, is Jesus.

Jesus, God's only Son, came to earth to be among people just like you. Jesus healed them, listened to them, taught them glorious secrets about His coming kingdom, and most of all, Jesus loved them. Jesus loved His people so much that He died for them and took the punishment for their sins. Jesus never sinned but was the perfect representation of God because Jesus is God.

Yet Jesus was punished like a criminal. His death paid the price of our sins. Now, those who trust in Jesus as their Savior are free from punishment and welcomed into God's family. The best news is that three days after Jesus died, He rose again and later took His throne in heaven. One day, Jesus will come back, wash the world of evil, and make the world His kingdom. This will be a place where there will be no tears, no fears, and no worries. There will be only peace and joyful praise because our Savior, King Jesus, holds the victory.

As we live our lives today, we wait excitedly for Jesus's kingdom to come. And while we wait, Jesus gives us a job to do! See, many people walk around in the dark. They do not know Jesus, and they do not know hope. Our job is to show them the light of Christ. This is called the Great Commission! Take a moment to read Matthew 28:18–20. Then, answer the question below.

1. What is our job as Christians?

2. Disciples are followers of Jesus. That means that if you love Jesus and follow Him, you are a disciple! Our job is to show others the love of Christ and share the good news of what He has done for us. Take a moment to brainstorm how you might make disciples in a few different spheres of your life: at your school, in your neighborhood, and among your friends.

   This may look like sharing your faith, caring for neighbors, inviting friends to church, serving at a homeless shelter, writing a "thank you" note, or baking cookies for someone in need of cheering up. The possibilities are endless!

3. Together with your discipleship leader, use the space below to make a plan to show Christ's love to someone in need throughout these spheres of your life within the next few weeks.

   SCHOOL:

   NEIGHBORHOOD:

   FRIENDS:

4. Want to remember the Great Commission? To help you, find the words from the Great Commission in the following word search. Once you find a word, circle or highlight it! Can you find them all?

```
S O N R B S H K P L R C S T B Y H U
X N N R O T E A R T H L N M E W O G
R B A W B A E D I S C I P L E S L O
B V T F S R U A L E F P O K G J Y C
R Y I T E L E T C R E L K L D Q S P
W F O C R L T M H H E A V E N D P F
I Y N N V W G U E O I P Z C X F I A
T B S L E H W M T M R N K B V X R T
H G Y Z R U Y G L X B I G Y M X I H
W B A P T I Z I N G U E T D R B T E
C O M M A N D E D G O O R Y T G W R
F F D U V T A L W A Y S R C B R S G
```

Find the following words in the puzzle.
Words are hidden ⇨ ⇩ and ⬊.

ALWAYS	EARTH	OBSERVE
AUTHORITY	FATHER	REMEMBER
BAPTIZING	HEAVEN	SON
COMMANDED	HOLY SPIRIT	TEACHING
DISCIPLES	NATIONS	WITH

Memorize the Great Commission! Can you use the words from the word search to fill in the blanks for Matthew 28:18–20?

Jesus came near and said to them, "All _____

has been given to me in _____ and on

_____ . Go, therefore, and make _____

of all _____ , _____ them in the

name of the _____ and of the _____ and

of the _____ _____ , _____

them to _____ everything I have _____

you. And _____ , I am _____ you _____ ,

to the end of the age."

God's greatest gift to us, by far, is Jesus.

Sharing the Good News of the Gospel with Students

Many people begin their relationship with Jesus at a young age. Throughout this study, the good news of the gospel is presented. Students may understand their sin and need for a Savior for the first time during this study. Discipleship leaders, you may want to ask your students if they want to decide to believe in Jesus and receive forgiveness for their sins. It is important not to pressure anyone to make this decision, but it is also important to lead them to Christ if they are ready.

We suggest asking your students the following questions to start a conversation about the gospel.

- What do you think about today's reading?
- Do you think Jesus died to forgive your sins?
- Are you ready to ask for forgiveness for your sins and tell Jesus you believe in Him?

Listen to your student's answers, and encourage them if they say they want to repent and believe. If your student expresses their belief in Jesus and a desire to trust Him as their Savior, you may want to help them communicate their repentance and belief to God.

When your student is ready to respond to the gospel message, there is no specific prayer to pray or formula to follow. Interestingly, the

Bible never actually presents us with a prayer that leads to salvation. Instead, Jesus often calls people to believe (John 6:35) and follow Him (Matthew 19:21). And the Apostle Paul teaches us to "confess with your mouth, 'Jesus is Lord,' and believe in your heart that God raised him from the dead" to be saved (Romans 10:9).

Scripture demonstrates that salvation is an issue of the heart. It is not the words you say but the belief in your heart that leads to salvation. Salvation is the work of God in response to one's faith in Christ.

However, a natural overflow of believing in God is praying to Him. And what better moment to pray to Him than in the moment you realize the depth of your sin and your need for a Savior? Praying with your student in response to the gospel is a sincere conversation between a repentant sinner and a gracious God, not a spoken script to receive salvation. However, you could lead them in a prayer that goes something like this:

> God, I've sinned against You, and I know that I can never make this right on my own. I trust that Jesus's sacrifice was enough to bring me into a real, life-changing relationship with You. Redeem my life, Lord. I cannot do it apart from You. I am making the choice to walk with You in my mind, heart, and actions every day, and I want to start today. Amen.

There is nothing magical about these words. They simply communicate the admission of sin and belief in God's saving power. Salvation is an issue of the heart.

If your student chooses to repent of their sin and believe in Jesus, celebrate this wonderful moment with them! Tell them they have made an amazing decision, and they are now part of God's family.

Salvation is the work of God in response to one's faith in Christ.

Tips for Helping Students Memorize Scripture

- Create actions to go along with each word or phrase.

- Practice a few times a day. Some great times to practice are during meals, in the car, and before bed.

- Write the first letter of each word in the verse on a sticky note, and use it as a cheat sheet until the verse is memorized.

- Post the verse in a visible place like the bathroom mirror or refrigerator.

- Sing the verse to the tune of a familiar song.

- Have students look up the verse in the Bible and read it independently.

- Keep track of verses memorized, and practice them once a week to promote long-term memory. Use resources from The Daily Grace Co.®, such as the *Scripture Memory Journal* or the *Daily He Leads Me Notepad*. You can find these resources at www.thedailygraceco.com.

Glossary

ADOPTION: Bringing the sinner into the family of God so that now God is his or her heavenly Father.

ATONEMENT: Christ accomplished salvation for God's people through His sinless life and obedient death on the cross.

AUTHORITY: The right to give orders and require obedience.

BIBLE: The holy, true, and authoritative Word of God.

CATEGORY: A group of people or things that share similar qualities.

CHARACTER: Traits or features that set a person apart.

FAITH: Trusting in Jesus and believing in His promises today.

GLORIFICATION: The end goal of every believer. Believers will be free from sin and will be transformed to have glorious bodies like Christ.

GOSPEL: The good news that salvation comes by grace alone through faith in Jesus Christ alone.

GRACE: The undeserved kindness of God toward the sinner.

HOLY: Moral wholeness and perfection; the absence of evil.

HOPE: To trust with confident expectation of good.

JUSTIFICATION: God declaring sinners not guilty.

MAN: Mankind was created in the image of God, but that image is stained by sin and can only be restored by Jesus's sacrifice on the cross.

PERSEVERANCE: Once someone begins to follow Christ, they will never stop believing in Him; their new life in Christ will continue into eternity.

REDEMPTION: Redemption is the sinner being freed from sin.

REGENERATION: An act of God in which He gives new spiritual life to His people.

REPENTANCE: Intentionally turning away from sin and turning toward God in obedience to His Word.

SANCTIFICATION: Growing more and more like Jesus through the power of the Holy Spirit.

THE FALL: Refers to Adam and Eve's disobedience in the garden of Eden through which sin entered the world.

THE FATHER: The first member of the Trinity. God is a Spirit who is infinite, eternal, and unchangeable. He is the One who initiates salvation. Salvation was His plan from eternity past.

THE HOLY SPIRIT: The third person of the Trinity who applies the work of salvation to the hearts of believers.

THEOLOGY: The study of God, His Word, and His works.

THE SON: The second person of the Trinity who accomplished salvation for sinners through His life and death.

THE TRINITY: The Trinity is the one true God in three persons—God the Father, the Son, and the Holy Spirit. All three persons of the Trinity are equal and eternal but have unique roles.

As we study the Bible, we get to know God and discover answers to some of our biggest questions.